WILLIAM "BILLY" CHAPPELL

1907-1994

FREDERIC A. SHARF

This publication was produced in support of two exhibitions. The fashion drawings are all exhibited in the **Sharf Admitting Center, Brigham and Women's Hospital**, 75 Francis Street, Boston. The ballet costume drawings are exhibited in the **Yawkey Center, Dana Farber Cancer Institute, Boston**, 450 Brookline Avenue, Boston

CONTENTS

▶ **Evening look costume design, tango velvet and trimmed sable**
MEDIUMS: Pencil, pen, brush, ink, watercolor and gouache / **DATE:** 1949

ACKNOWLEDGEMENTS

The biography of William "Billy" Chappell could never have been assembled without some valuable assistance:

To begin with I am indebted to the eagle eye of my London friend **Philip Athill** who acquired the group of 90 Chappell drawings for me at a British auction.

Once I realized that I would need knowledge of the ballet scene in England during Chappell's life I needed to turn to my friends at **Sotheran's** in London and **Argosy** in New York City. These two shops, both dealers in out-of-print books, tracked down books which were invaluable in providing the background details.

Chappell's close association with key people in the evolution of British ballet,—in particular **Frederick Ashton** and **Margot Fonteyn**,—enabled me to tease out factual information about Chappell from accounts of their lives.

My trusted designer **Paul Cyr** worked with me to put drawings and text into meaningful placement.

I could never have created the text without the help of **Margie Phillips** in my office.

After acquiring the drawings I met with **Chris Collins** of the Brigham and Women's Hospital, **Elaine Tinetti** and **Lydia Lopoukhine** of the Dana-Farber Cancer Institute in order to divide the group into two exhibitions. **Jane Mayer** was helpful in adding her stamp of approval to the Dana-Farber selection.

Editorial support was provided by **Laura G. Strauss**

The daunting job of organizing framing and installation was handled smoothly by **Mark Wallison**.

This publication was printed and bound by Velocity Print Solutions, Middlebury, CT

ISBN-10: 099-03152-7-4
ISBN-13: 978-0-9903152-7-8

Library of Congress Control Number: A catalog record for this book is available from the Library of Congress.

FIRST EDITION
Printed in the United States of America

OPENING

PRINCIPAL

Chappell
1942

WILLIAM "BILLY" CHAPPELL
1907-1994

INTRODUCTION

For the first thirty years of the 20th century, ballet in Great Britain was confined to visits from important European dance companies, of which Diaghilev's Ballet Russes was the star attraction. Occasionally, a home grown talent emerged, such as the Jewish girl Alice Marks who was good enough to join Diaghilev, but only after changing her name to Alicia Markova.

On 19th of August 1929 Diaghilev died. His ballet troupe scattered. His dancers began to join new companies, primarily based in Monte Carlo. In England, opportunity existed to develop indigenous ballet companies and produce British ballet stars. During the decade of the 1930s, ballet in England flourished. Celebrated international stars emerged, such as Margot Fonteyn and Frederick Ashton.

William Chappell, known to his friends as Billy, was a major presence in the evolution of British ballet in the 1930s. He danced with Ashton and Fonteyn. He created scenery and costumes for various British ballet companies. Gradually, the center of the ballet world moved from Paris and Monte Carlo to London during this decade. Billy was on the ground floor of this shift.

He was talented and personable. He was a close friend of most of the people who were the leaders of this shift. Yet, he remains today only a footnote in the history of British ballet.

◄ Costume design for Dorothy Dickson
MEDIUMS: Pencil, brush and gouache / DATE: 1942

PAGES 4-5 Design Drawing for a London Stage Set
In the autumn of 1957 Chappell was hired to direct a new London musical "Expresso Bongo." The show opened on April 23,1958 at the Saville Theatre in the West End of London. While it was well received, it went up against another London musical "My Fair Lady." Chappell's stage setting and overall directing helped to give "Expresso Bongo" a decent run. The plot was gritty, the setting contemporary and the music pop. In 1959, it was made into a movie.

FREDERIC A. SHARF

WILLIAM "BILLY" CHAPPELL
1907-1994

British Ballet Dancer, 1930s | Couturier to London Café Society, 1940s | Designer of Costumes for Ballet & Theatre, 1930-1980

I

William Chappell was born on September 27, 1907 in the Staffordshire city of Wolverhampton. His father was in the theatre business; his mother was involved with the fashion world. When he was young his parents divorced. Billy moved with his mother and sister to London. He later described his childhood house as a "semi-detached home in a shabby suburb of London,"—Balham, near Wandsworth.

In January 1921 his mother enrolled him in the Chelsea School of Art. Somehow she realized that his future would lie in the arts. He quickly fell in with a small group of talented pupils. Edward Burra would go on to a distinguished career as a painter. Barbara Ker-Seymer became a renown photographer and Clover Pritchard completed the quartet. They were a group apart and they remained lifelong friends.

Chappell's first friend, Edward Burra, was his most important friend. Burra introduced Billy to an entirely different way of life. He came from the upper sector of British society. His family resided in a mansion in the south coast city of Rye. Chappell went there frequently. The premises made an impression on him: the house had two housemaids and a cook; the extensive grounds were cared for by two gardeners and a handyman.

Backed by Burra's family wealth, Billy and Ed began to move on the edge of fashionable London society, —a group called by Noel Coward "Bright Young People." This group held fancy dress parties that lasted until early morning hours. Dancing was an essential part of these parties, especially the newest American dance, the Charleston. Costumes were another essential ingredient of these parties.

◀ **Stork ballet costume**
MEDIUMS: Pencil, pen, brush, ink, watercolor and gouache / **DATE:** 1948

In 1925 Burra's father paid for Billy and Ed to travel to Paris to see Josephine Baker perform. They were under close supervision by two teachers at Chelsea School of Art. This experience marked the beginning of both Billy and Ed's lifetime interest in contemporary black culture.

Chappell's interests soon moved from the fine arts to dance. He spent the summer of 1926 in Ostende, Belgium, with a female friend in a cabaret dance act. Billy was very handsome, and always well dressed. Girls fell hard for him, but he had no romantic interest in girls.

Meanwhile, ballet was bubbling up in London. Marie Rambert opened a British ballet entitled "A Tragedy of Fashion" at the Lyric Theatre, Hammersmith in which she introduced a new dancer, Frederick Ashton, and a new designer of scenery and costumes, Sophie Fedorovitch. This ballet opened June 15, 1926. It was a success. Marie wanted another male dancer to pair with Ashton.

Marie Rambert was convinced that Chappell's ballroom dance skills could be translated into ballet. She introduced Ashton and Fedorovitch to Billy and Ed and Barbara Ker-Seymer. They became social friends and Billy learned ballet dancing. By the end of 1927 Billy was good enough to be hired with Ashton to dance with the Royal Opera at Covent Garden. They opened in April 1928.

In the audience was Ninette de Valois. She was born in Ireland and named Edris Stannus but changed her name when she joined Diaghilev in 1923. She was hoping to start her own dance company in London. She liked the high spirits and inventive fun of the two young dancers Ashton and Chappell; she went back stage after the performance to interview them. She hoped they would come on board when her dance company was finally formed.

By the end of 1927 Chappell was a ballet dancer on the one hand and a member of the "Bright Young People" on the other. New Year's Eve 1927 he spent attending an elaborate costume party at Albert Hall,—the annual New Years Eve Chelsea Arts Ball. Billy came with Barbara Ker-Seymer in identical fishnet costumes that Billy had created. In May 1928 he attended a lavish party thrown by a prominent producer of theatrical dance acts. On July 10, 1928 Billy danced with Ashton in a charity matinee performance of a new ballet created by Ashton entitled "Leda and the Swan." Once again they were sensational!

Chappell was unable to put aside the social fun available as the Jazz Age entered its final year in 1928. He seems to have spent his time attending costume parties, dancing with Ashton and vacationing in France with Burra. He planned to join Burra in Toulon in the south of France for the summer of 1928.

Meanwhile, Ashton had decided to join a new European dance company assembled by Ida Rubinstein to compete with Diaghilev. Rehearsals started on August 1st,1928 in Paris. Performances would start in November in Paris, followed by a four month tour of major cities in Europe. Ashton convinced his friend Billy to audition, and he was accepted in August 1928. Burra accompanied Billy to the audition.

Chappell and Ashton roomed together in Paris. Rehearsals were very tiring, leaving them with little time to enjoy being in Paris. The star of the company was the Russian ballerina Nijinska. Les Ballets de Mme Ida Rubinstein opened at the end of November 1928. The four month tour of Europe started in January 1929. The pay was poor and living conditions were spartan. By the spring of 1929 Ashton and Billy had had enough. Marie Rambert wanted them back in London.

Marie Rambert and her husband Ashley Dukes, a writer, had transformed an old church at Notting Hill Gate into a small theatre which they named the Mercury Theatre. She decided to stage a new ballet which Ashton would choreograph entitled "Capriol Suite." Chappell was assigned the task of creating scenery and costumes for the ballet. Performances in 1930 made Ashton a star, and launched Billy as "a gifted stage designer."

▲ **William Chappell and Diane Gould** / 1931

III

Serious ballet in London was at a low point by the end of 1929. Serious ballet elsewhere in England was non existent. However, the ballet landscape was about to be altered in the early thirties by three factors.

At a dinner party in London on 16 February 1930 a small group of dedicated ballet fans decided to form a Society to encourage the development of British talent by financially backing performances. The Camargo Society, named for a legendary ballerina, was created by the well known conductor Constant Lambert, and the retired ballerina Lydia Lopokova. Lydia's husband John Maynard Keynes, the internationally famous economist, was treasurer of the new venture. Their objective was to rent West End theatres on Sunday evenings and Monday matinees performances.

Meanwhile, Marie Rambert had transformed her ballet dance school into a proper dance company, with "Capriol Suite" as their inaugural production. Ashton and Chappell were her star dancers; and the Camargo Society intended to steal them for their performances. Thus, by the middle of 1930 there were two active ballet companies in London.

The final factor was provided by Ninette de Valois when she created the Vic-Wells Ballet in 1931. Performances would be held at two famous London theatres,—the Old Vic and the Sadler's Wells. Her first ballet performance opened at the Old Vic on 5th May 1931. The New Sadler's Wells Theatre had opened on 6th January 1931.

It was not easy to make a living from ballet in the early 1930s. Billy and Ashton worked for three dance companies, and from time to time performed in musical reviews held in traditional theatres. Chappell designed scenery and costume for all three companies.

In the summer of 1931 Chappell and Ashton took a break from the dance world. They vacationed at Toulon in the south of France. They slept together in a double bed to save money, but they were not romantically involved. Ed Burra was with them, as was the London playboy Bunny Roger. Barbara Ker-Seymer came, as did Sophie Fedorovitch. Each night they would dress up in costume, usually as sailors. It is no accident that Ashton's next ballet creation was entitled "Regatta" with a nautical theme and costumes by Billy.

IV

After returning from their vacation at Toulon, Ashton and Chappell were occupied with numerous dance projects. In February 1931, Ashton's ballet "La Peri" opened at the Mercury Theatre. Ashton and Markova danced the lead roles. Chappell designed the scenery and costumes. Later that month the Camargo Society produced "Capriol Suite" with Ashton and Chappell as lead dancers. At the end of April the Camargo Society introduced Ashton's masterpiece "Façade." Chappell did not design scenery or costumes but did perform lead roles in several scenes.

In November 1931 Ashton's ballet "Regatta" opened at the Old Vic Theatre. Chappell designed scenery and costumes which were based on their previous summer's experience at Toulon. In addition, he was one of the featured dancers. At the end of 1931 the Camargo Society produced another Ashton ballet entitled "Rio Grande." Chappell danced the lead role as a Creole Boy; Markova danced the lead female role as Creole Girl. Chappell's best friend Edward Burra designed the scenery and costumes.

In June 1932 the Camargo Society produced a new ballet entitled "High Yellow." Chappell designed the scenery and costumes with the well known artist Vanessa Bell. Ashton designed the choreography with assistance from an African-American dancer, —an initial mixture of the negro dance world with ballet. The British intellectuals were attracted to the writers and artists of the Harlem Renaissance, and the artists of Mexico. In 1934 Edward Burra traveled to both Harlem and Mexico.

Ballet was now flourishing in London. Between the Camargo Society, the Vic-Wells Ballet, and Madame Rambert's Ballet Club Chappell was kept busy as a dancer and designer. His costume designs now required new creativity as the ballet settings moved to more exotic locations.

The Camargo Society felt that they had achieved their ballet objective and their treasurer John Maynard Keynes pointed out that they had accumulated debts while pursuing their mission. Therefore, in mid-June 1933 they held one final production at a West End theatre to clear their debts.

Early in 1934 Chappell was busy rehearsing with Ninette de Valois for the premiere of a new ballet "The Haunted Ballroom" which would star the Australian dancer Robert Helpmann with Alicia Markova. Billy had a leading role, and de Valois would later write "William Chappell gave a strong and sensitive performance as the Stranger Player who controls the action." Among the corps de ballet was a teenage protege of de Valois, Margot Fonteyn née Peggy Hookham.

▲ Alicia Markova and Frederick Ashton (center) in LA PÉRI / 1931

In 1933 Ninette de Valois added a new young client to the Vic-Wells Ballet school. Her name, Peggy Hookham, was not deemed suitable for a future ballerina. After much discussion with her mother, and after several interim names, a final name was selected,—Margot Fonteyn. Chappell met the teenager in 1933. His first impression was that she was "an annoyingly self-possessed child." In fact she was very shy, and somewhat intimidated by the older dancers. Her best friend among the dancers was Pamela May.

In July 1933 a new ballet company, assembled in Europe by Colonel W. de Basil, opened at the Alhambra Theatre in London. The company name was Ballets Russes de Monte-Carlo, and the dancers were primarily Russian. They were well received by the London audiences. De Basil had come up with the idea of featuring "baby ballerinas," two Russian teenagers,—one was 14 and the other 16. The company had been booked to stay for three weeks in July but the response was so positive that they stayed until early November.

In 1934 the company returned, now at the Royal Opera House, opening June 19th. By the time they ended their London run in August 1934 the dancers were well known in London. They were pampered by affluent admirers, and they attended dinner parties, weekend house-parties, and charity balls.

Ninette de Valois noted the attention received by de Basil's "baby ballerinas" —a third teenager was added for the 1934 production, and decided it was time to launch her own teenager Margot Fonteyn. Her role in "The Haunted Ballroom," also a 1934 production, was the beginning of an extraordinary career,

Margot and Chappell spent a lot of time together during rehearsals for "The Haunted Ballroom," and while Billy recalled that "we were chums," Fonteyn developed a teenage crush on the handsome Chappell. De Valois decided to have Ashton create a revised version of his 1931 hit "Rio Grande" which would open in the fall of 1935 at the Sadler's Wells Theatre. When Markova refused to play the Creole Girl again, the role was given to Fonteyn. Billy would once again play the role of Creole Boy. Margot Fonteyn would later recall that her crush on Billy "coincided with rehearsals .... Billy was a sailor and I the girl he picked

▲ Diana Gould, with Frederick Ashton and William Chappell / 1931

up .... I was provided most opportunely with an excuse to regard him affectionately while acting my role." She had no idea that Billy was gay.

Fonteyn's performance in "Rio Grande" launched her as a prima ballerina. Meanwhile, Alicia Markova who had turned down the role decided in 1935 to break away from Vic-Wells and form her own company with Anton Dolin. She had financial backing to create a new version of "Giselle" the ballet for which she was most well known. She would later write that "the talents of William Chappell were engaged" to create scenery and costumes for their opening at the Shaftsbury Theatre in London, to be followed by a provincial tour of major cities in England and Scotland.

By 1936 British ballet companies were the equal of any of the European companies. Chappell was now equally important as a dancer and a designer. His services in both capacities were much in demand. London was

▲ **William Chappell in THE PLANETS** / 1934

engaged on all sides with plans for the Coronation year in 1937. Ashton created a new ballet entitled "Les Patineurs" which would open in April 1937, for which Chappell would design scenery and costumes. Billy did not dance in this production.

In 1937 the Vic-Wells Ballet was invited to Paris to represent England at the International Exhibition of Arts and Industry, —the major World's Fair of that year. They performed the ballet "Checkmate" on June 1, 1937 at the Theatre des Champs-Elysees. Billy was one of the feature dancers, playing the role of a Red Knight. Scenery and costumes were designed by the celebrated industrial designer E. McKnight Kauffer.

In the fall of 1937 Chappell danced at the Sadler's Wells Theatre in another Ashton ballet entitled "A Wedding Bouquet;" and he created new scenery and costumes for a revised version of Ashton's 1933 hit "Les Rendezvous," In the spring of 1938 Chappell worked on designs for a new Ashton ballet entitled "Judgment of Paris" and he would rehearse for his role as Mercury in that ballet.

At the end of August 1939 the Vic-Wells Ballet Company began their scheduled tour of provincial English cities. A number of different ballets were performed, of which "Swan Lake" was the most loved. On the morning of September 3,1939 they traveled from Manchester to Leeds. When they arrived at the Leeds train station, Chappell saw from his train window a porter walking along the platform repeating "War's been declared."

The company was immediately disbanded. Chappell, Ashton, and Helpmann went to stay with Doris Langley Moore in Harrogate, about ten miles from Leeds. She was a wealthy fashion historian, and a friend of Edward Burra. She was famous for her hospitality, even writing a book entitled "The Pleasure of Your Company" which was a guide to stylish entertaining. Billy illustrated this book. After a few days Ashton, Helpmann, and Billy went to the Isle of Wight to stay with Helpmann's aunt. On the 17th of September Ashton was able to regroup the ballet company. Billy decided not to accompany them. He was the first male ballet dancer to sign up for military service.

VII

Chappell signed up for service in the Royal Artillery. He reported early in 1940. He was sent to Brighton to await a potential German invasion. Edward Burra was able to visit him, and they had coffee at a local cafe. In 1941 Chappell was transferred to Larkhill, a garrison town about ten miles from Salisbury.

Billy trained as a gunner, but was given preferential treatment. He was deemed "useful" for his ability to organize entertainment for the troops; and for his artistic skills. He put on musical reviews. He was allowed to create modernist murals in communal rooms. Burra wrote Ashton that Billy was having such a good time that he might go on forever.

Meanwhile he was selected for officer training (OCTU) and transferred to Ilkley, Yorkshire in the spring of 1942. There he endured lengthy marches, and studied anti-tank training. He was promoted from Gunner to Second Lieutenant. In May 1943 he was at a base near Tunbridge-Wells.

While most English bases were involved in the build-up towards D-Day, Billy was destined to go to the Italian front. Burra wrote to Billy on March 28, 1944 in Naples, addressing him as Captain Chappell. He spent the balance of 1944 and most of 1945 in Naples.

Burra tried to keep Chappell informed about the ballet business in England, but it appears that Billy was shifting his interests from ballet to theatre; —from dancing to theatrical design. He wrote to Burra at the end of 1945 that he was in the process of opening a "theatrical dress-makers and designing business in Bruton Place."

Surviving drawings indicate that Chappell used his spare time in the army to continue designing costumes, and even to create designs which could become couture. However, he needed some financial backing to consider opening his own establishment. Captain Chappell in Naples, Italy would never have been able to negotiate premises, and setup a work force without somebody in London organizing these details.

The likely "somebody" was his old friend Bunny Roger. Neil "Bunny" Roger was the Oxford educated son of a wealthy self-made Scottish entrepreneur. Even while studying at Oxford Bunny was determined to make his own fortune by designing clothes. In 1937 he opened a dress-making establishment on Great Newport Street. His clients were drawn from the upper levels of British society, and included theatrical stars like Vivien Leigh. When the war ended he setup shop in Bruton Place. When Chappell returned from military service, he moved into these premises.

VIII

In 1946, as if by magic, Captain William Chappell, having served nearly six years in the British Army, turned himself into a London couturier. He was located in Mayfair, the very smartest address for such a business, at No. 40 Bruton Place. While telling his friends he was simply a "theatrical dressmaker" he began designing day dresses, evening gowns, and even swimwear for an elite group of clients, many of them dancers that he had worked with in the 1930s.

His partner Bunny Roger was certainly able to bring in wealthy ladies who did not need to worry about ration coupons. However, Billy's 1946 designs looked like re-treads of wartime clothing. In February 1947 they became completely outdated when Christian Dior launched his "New Look" in Paris.

It seems that Bunny soon lost faith in Billy, and became convinced that Billy was out of the couture league. In addition, Bunny wanted to make a big financial hit, and realized he would never do that with Billy. He looked around the London couture scene and spotted Hardy Amies as a high level couture talent whose business was in need of cash.

Sometime in 1949 Bunny jumped ship. By 1950 he was listed as an investor in Hardy Amies Ltd, with offices on Saville Row. Bunny took over the ground floor office which Amies had originally occupied. His investment paid off in 1973 when Debenhams acquired the House of Amies.

Meanwhile, Billy turned his attention to the business he knew best:—costume design. In 1949 his friend Frederick Ashton asked Billy to recreate the original designs for scenery and costumes for "Façade," an Ashton ballet in which Billy had danced when the ballet was first produced in 1931. On March 2, 1950 "Façade" opened at the Royal Opera House. Billy was given no credit for his efforts.

▲ William Chappell and W. Gore in FAÇADE / 1931

In 1950 Chappell was asked by a London publisher to write a book about his friend Margot Fonteyn. The publisher had an extensive series of books on "Theatre, Plays & Players" but the publisher had no book on ballet, which had become a popular art form in post-war England. Chappell did not want to write a biography. His book was simply entitled "Fonteyn: Impressions of a Ballerina."

Chappell brought in as a collaborator his long-time friend Cecil Beaton, a distinguished photographer. Beaton did a series of photos showing Fonteyn in some of her famous roles and, in addition, some casual shots in her dressing room. None of the 40 photos in Chappell's book had ever been published before. The text was illustrated with charming drawings by Chappell. A deluxe edition of 250 copies was produced, each book signed by Fonteyn and Chappell.

On 15 May 1950 a Gala Performance took place at the Sadler's Wells Theatre to celebrate the twenty-first anniversary of their Ballet Company. Ninette de Valois, who had founded this company, invited Chappell to dance in that Gala. She asked him to select one of his signature roles from the 1930s. He selected the role he had played in the "Popular Song" sequence from "Façade." Chappell attended three strenuous rehearsals. At the end of the third rehearsal he tore a calf muscle and was forced to watch the Gala from a seat in the audience. His days as a ballet dancer were clearly at an end!

IX

Chappell transformed himself from a successful ballet dancer, and a much admired designer of ballet scenery and costume into a successful director of musical reviews in the 1950s. In 1953 he directed "High Spirits" with Cyril Ritchard and Diana Churchill at the London Hippodrome. His friend Barbara Ker-Seymer raved about the production in a letter to Edward Burra. They were both proud of what their childhood friend was achieving in his new career.

A musical review entitled "The Lyric Review" ran for three seasons at two London theatres during the 1950s. In 1956 he directed a Sheridan revival and a Noel Coward play with Vivien Leigh. In 1958/1959 he directed the Frank Loesser musical "Where's Charley?"

While there was triumph on the London stage, there was sadness in Chappell's personal life. Sophie Fedorovitch, a member of his student group, died suddenly on February 3rd 1953. This was a particularly devastating blow to Frederick Ashton for whom Sophie had designed scenery and costumes for eleven of his ballets. Billy sat up all night until 3am the next morning consoling Ashton.

Billy became well known in show business circles. In 1961 he began work with Orson Wells on a movie "The Trial." He was given a role in the movie as the artist Titorelli. Production began in Zagreb, Yugoslavia. Early in 1962 he was living in Rome with Orson and Paola Wells. Chappell traveled with the actors in 1962 as filming sequences were made in Paris, Dubrovnik, Milan and Rome. Edward Burra commented in a letter "you do seem to be moving in high circles." He became quite friendly with the movie's star Anthony Perkins.

On October 24th, 1970 Chappell's oldest and closest friend Edward Burra died. Billy would ultimately create two volumes of letters and tributes to Burra. They had maintained a lifelong correspondence, and Burra had saved all the letters. In fact, Burra had corresponded extensively with all of the Chelsea Art School group

The Royal Ballet was planning a Farewell Tribute to Frederick Ashton on 24 July 1970. The contents were a secret from Ashton. Billy was in charge of writing the commentary which would link the various tributes. He decided to stay with Barbara Ker-Seymer at her Islington home. Ashton called repeatedly to find out the details but Barbara refused to let him speak with Billy.

The event covered forty years of Ashton's life in ballet. The opening dance was from "Capriol Suite" which Ashton had choreographed in 1930. Dance pieces from the next forty years followed. When it ended Ashton was too emotional to stand and speak.

On the 18th of May 1979 the Royal Opera House held a celebration in honor of Margot Fonteyn's 60th birthday. Dame Margot asked her old flame Billy to design the dress she would wear to this event. When the various performances ended, the curtain rose for the audience to see Fonteyn seated on stage wearing the calf-length evening dress of oyster-shell pink designed by Billy.

A special tribute was being organized to celebrate the 80th birthday of Queen Elizabeth The Queen Mother. The event was to take place on 4th August 1980. Ashton was asked to choreograph a new ballet which he titled "Rhapsody." The World Premiere of "Rhapsody" took place that night with Her Majesty present. Choreography and scenery were designed by Ashton. The costumes were designed by Chappell. Everyone agreed that Chappell's costumes were too ornate. Ashton attempted to make changes. Chappell was unhappy with the proposed changes. They communicated by notes. In the end Ashton decided not to hurt Billy's feelings. Lesley Collier and Mikhail Baryshnikov were the stars; the costumes were credited to William Chappell. Ashton and Chappell quickly made peace. Every night for the rest of his life Ashton would phone Chappell.

Ashton died on August 18, 1988. Billy was too sick to attend the funeral. However, he was able to pay his respects three months later on November 29, 1988, at a Thanksgiving Service at Westminster Abbey. The Queen Mother, Princess Margaret, and stars from the Royal Ballet attended. There was no such tribute to William "Billy" Chappell when he died on 1st January 1994.

▶ **Ballet costume for the Principal Dancer in "Madame Butterfly"**
MEDIUMS: Pencil, ink and watercolor / **DATE:** 1948

▲ **Scarf detail / Les Patineurs** / **DATE:** 1948
Vic-Wells Ballet Company at Sadler's Wells Theatre, April 27, 1937
Scenery and Costumes by William Chappell
Choreography by Frederick Ashton

▲ **Scarf detail / Les Sylphides** / **DATE:** 1948
A production associated with Alicia Markova and Ninette de Valois
Margot Fonteyn danced in late 1946 movie for kids entitled "The Little Ballerina."

CORNFIELD.

PRINCIPAL DANCER
AS BUTTERFLY

WILLIAM "BILLY" CHAPPELL
1907-1994

POST WWII COUTURE DREAMS

While spending six years in military service, Chappell had time to draw, and to dream. He knew his dancing days were over. He believed he could leverage his design talents to create up-market ladies clothing.

In Britain he faced rationing of fabrics; restrictions on such details as pleats, pockets, buttons. On the other hand British women wanted to look glamorous; even during the war years they made the best use of whatever was available.

Chappell's 1946 creations were an extension of 1930s fashion. Broad shoulders and small waists; evening gowns styled from Hollywood movies; knee length skirts. This look might have survived if Christian Dior did not change the entire game.

By the summer of 1946 word leaked out of Paris that Dior had financial backing to establish his own House, and he was planning to launch a new collection early in 1947. On February 12th, 1947 his new collection was shown to the fashion world, and was dubbed the "New Look".

Dior designed dresses that accented the female figure: dresses were longer and skirts fuller; shoulders were soft, not boxy; busts were prominent and waists narrow. Female curves were important to the "New Look."

In general, British designers were slow to adopt this look, in part because of government restrictions, and in part because tradition still meant a lot to British women. But the big, established couture Houses in London could react more cautiously. They had large customer bases, and were well financed. The day of the small, luxury craft couture House was ending. Billy was in the wrong place at the wrong time.

Chappell never stopped designing dresses for a handful of special clients, such as Margot Fonteyn. However, as Fonteyn became an international star she turned to the Paris couture Houses for most of her attire. He seems to have access to cutting and sewing staff until 1980, but he never succeeded in establish a Chappell brand.

DESIGN DRAWINGS
COUTURE

Black wool crepe dress designed for Pamela May
MEDIUMS: Pencil, brush and ink / DATE: 1946

PAMELA MAY : **Pamela May, OBE**, (1917-2005) danced with Chappell from 1934 -1939. She danced with the Royal Ballet until 1952, as a Principal Dancer, and thereafter until 1982 in character roles.

Silk linen Summer suits for Miss Pamela May
MEDIUMS: Pencil, pen, brush, ink, watercolor and gouache on grey paper / **DATE:** 1946

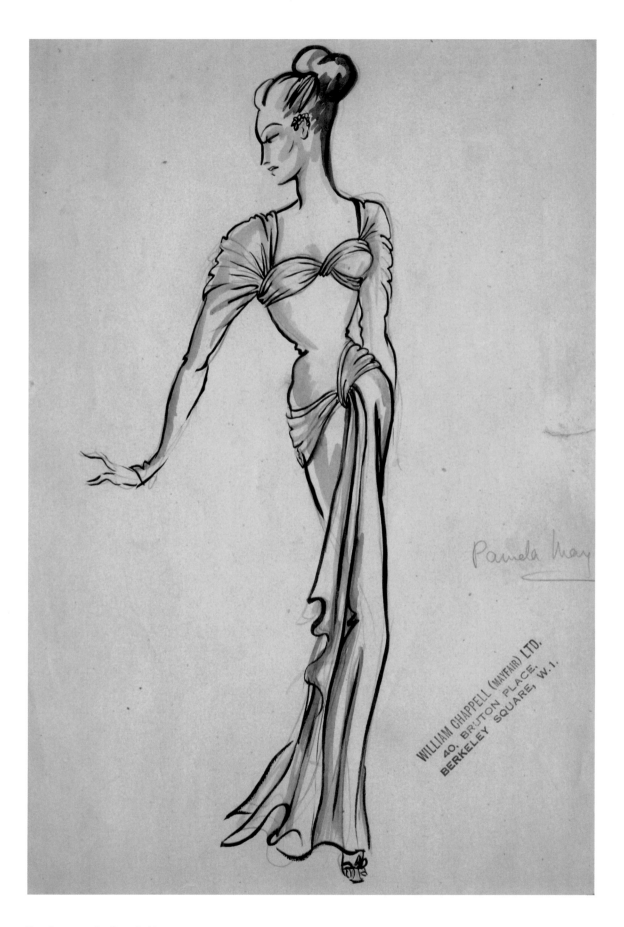

WILLIAM CHAPPELL (MAYFAIR) LTD.
40, BRUTON PLACE,
BERKELEY SQUARE, W.1.

Pamela May

Evening gown for Pamela May
MEDIUMS: Pencil, brush and ink / **DATE:** 1946

WILLIAM CHAPPELL (MAYFAIR) **LTD.**

DOROTHY DICKSON

Evening suit and earring design for Dorothy Dickson
MEDIUMS: Pencil, ink and gouache on grey paper / **DATE:** 1946

Dorothy Dickson (1893-1995) was born in the United States. She began her career as an actress in silent films before moving to England in the 1920s where she became a stage star, as well as a close friend of the future Queen Elizabeth. Chappell became friendly with her in the late 1930s and began to design stage costumes for her to wear while touring British troop camps during the war.

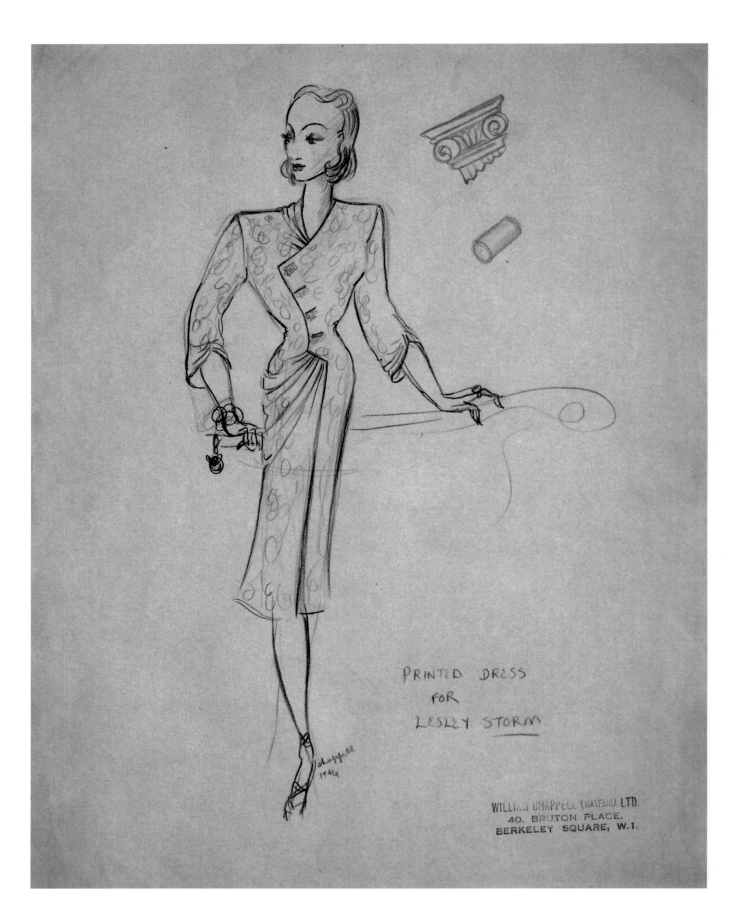

PRINTED DRESS
FOR
LESLEY STORM

WILLIAM CHAPPELL (MAYFAIR) LTD.
40. BRUTON PLACE.
BERKELEY SQUARE, W.1.

Printed dress for Lesley Storm
MEDIUMS: Pencil and crayons on grey paper / **DATE:** 1946

LESLEY STORM : **Lesley Storm** (1898-1975) was the pen-name of the Scottish writer Mabel Cowie. She was well known for stage plays, some of which became movies. She also wrote novels.

Printed dress and jacket for Lesley Storm
MEDIUMS: Pencil and crayons on grey paper / DATE: 1946

BEACH CLOTHES
FOR
FONTEYN

Beach clothes for Margo Fonteyn
MEDIUMS: Pencil, brush and watercolor on grey paper / **DATE:** 1946

MARGOT FONTEYN : **Dame Margot Fonteyn, DBE** (1919-1991) was England's leading ballerina from 1935 until 1979. She was one of Chappell's closest personal friends.

Afternoon Dress for Margot Fonteyn
MEDIUMS: Pencil, pen, brush and ink / **DATE:** 1946

Evening dress for Margot Fonteyn
MEDIUMS: Pencil, brush and ink / DATE: Circa 1948

Design for an evening dress (probable client: Margo Fonteyn)
MEDIUMS: Pencil, Pen, brush, ink and watercolor / **DATE:** Circa 1946-1948

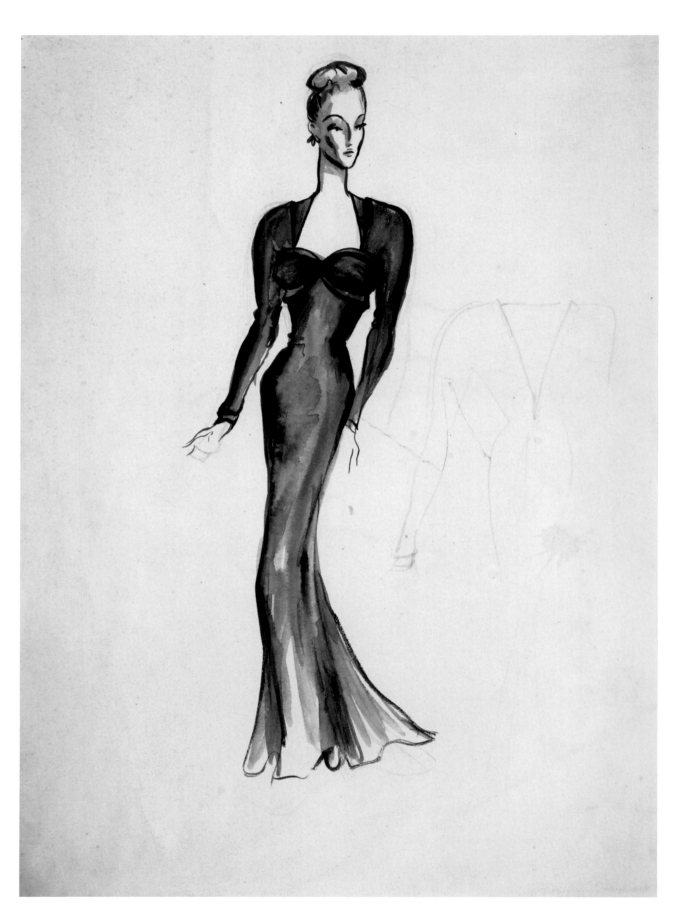

Design for an evening dress (probable client: Margo Fonteyn)
MEDIUMS: Pencil, brush and ink / **DATE:** Circa 1946-1948

Design for an evening dress (probable client: Margo Fonteyn)
MEDIUMS: Pencil, pen, brush and ink / **DATE:** Circa 1946-1948

MRS. MAX AITKEN

Mrs. Aitken was second wife of 2nd Baronet Max Aitken. In 1946 Max went into the family business, the Daily Express Newspaper. Aitken divorced his first wife in 1944, and married Jane Kenyon-Slaney in 1946. They had two daughters and divorced in 1950.

Mrs. Aitken was the perfect socialite which Chappell wanted to attract. She was probably a friend of Bunny Roger.

Mrs. Aitken was very well connected. Her father-in-law, Lord Beaverbrook, not only owned one of Britain's most influential newspapers, but was a close friend of Sir Winston Churchill.

Black evening gown designed for Mrs. Aitken
MEDIUMS: Pencil, pen, brush and ink / DATE: 1948

Black day dress designed for Mrs. Aitken
MEDIUMS: Pencil, pen, brush and ink / DATE: Circa 1946-1948

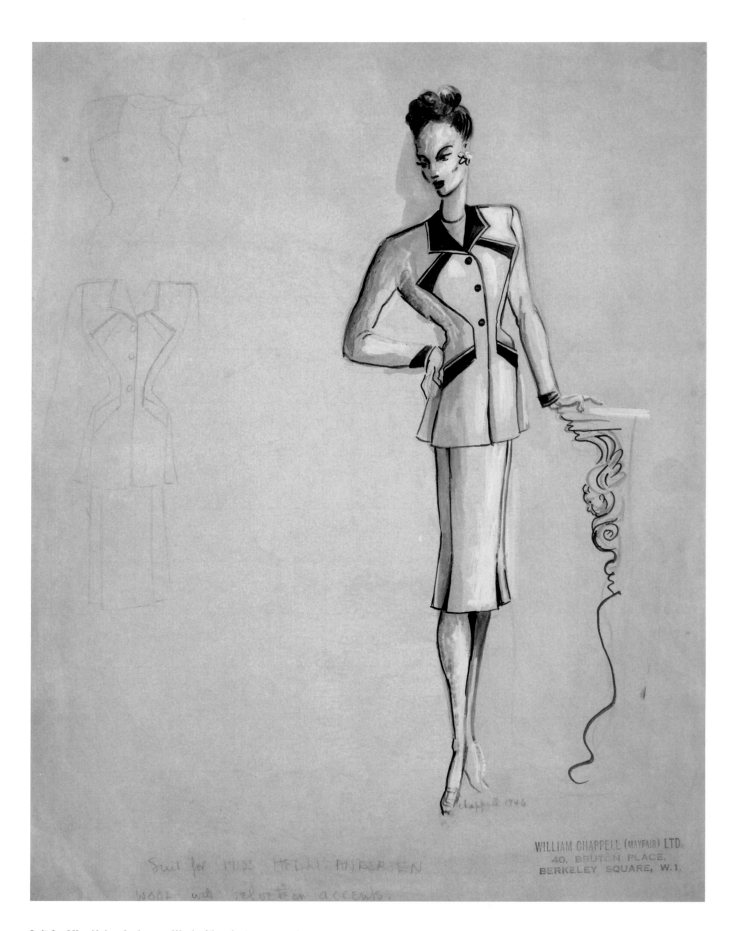

Suit for Miss Helen Andersen. Wool with velveteen accents
MEDIUMS: Pencil, pen, brush, ink, watercolor and gouache on grey paper / DATE: 1946

Cocktail dress designed for Mrs. Gasener
MEDIUMS: Pencil, pen, brush and ink / **DATE:** Circa 1946-1948

Design for a draped evening dress
MEDIUMS: Pencil, pen, brush, ink and gouache on grey paper / DATE: Circa 1946-1948

White crepe dinner dress
MEDIUMS: Pencil, brush and ink on grey paper / DATE: 1946

Black Ottoman silk Ascot suit with stylish wide-brimmed hat
MEDIUMS: Pencil, pen, brush, ink and watercolor on grey paper / DATE: 1946

Three draped dresses
MEDIUMS: Pencil, ink and watercolor on grey paper / DATE: Circa 1946-1948

Dinner dress. Draped black skirt with contrast bodice. Or: Black sweater top with jet collar and jet fringes at sleeves
MEDIUMS: Pencil, pen, brush, ink, watercolor and gouache on grey paper / DATE: 1946

EVENING DRESS - in CORDED SILK.

WILLIAM CHAPPELL (MAYFAIR) LTD.
40. BRUTON PLACE.
BERKELEY SQUARE, W.1.

Evening Dress in corded silk
MEDIUMS: Pencil, watercolor and gouache on grey paper / **DATE:** 1946

Bathing suit in emerald and turquoise (and) Coolie coat in emerald and turquoise
MEDIUMS: Pencil, pen, ink, watercolor and gouache on grey paper / DATE: 1946

Design for an evening dress
MEDIUMS: Pencil, brush and watercolor / DATE: Circa 1946-1948

Evening dress
MEDIUMS: Brush and ink / **DATE:** Circa 1946-1948

Grey linen and white piqué version I
MEDIUMS: Pencil, pen, ink, watercolor and gouache on grey paper / **DATE:** 1946

Grey linen and white piqué version II
MEDIUMS: Pencil, pen, ink, watercolor and gouache on grey paper / DATE: 1946

Design in grey linen and white pique version III
MEDIUMS: Pencil, pen, ink, watercolor and gouache on grey paper / **DATE:** 1946

Design for a cocktail dress, I
MEDIUMS: Pencil, brush and gouache / **DATE:** Circa 1946-1948

Design for a cocktail dress, II
MEDIUMS: Pencil, brush and gouache / DATE: Circa 1946-1948

Design for a cocktail dress, III
MEDIUMS: Pencil, brush and gouache / DATE: Circa 1946-1948

Design for a cocktail dress, IV
MEDIUMS: Pencil, brush and gouache / **DATE:** Circa 1946-1948

DESIGN DRAWINGS
COSTUME

◀ **Scarf design detail of the Royal Opera House depicting the house as seen from the perspective of the cast.**
Royal Opera House reopened February 1946 with performance by Sadler's Wells Ballet Company. This ballet company became the Royal Ballet in 1956. Covent Garden site then housed both Royal Opera and Royal Ballet. During WWII the building was a dance hall.

PUNCH
AND JUDY 1948

A traditional British puppet show, normally performed at fair grounds...The characters were well known to any British audience.

Mr. Punch, his wife Judy, their Baby, Toby the Dog, and the Policeman were among the usual cast of characters. Lesser characters were included at the discretion of the performer.

The audience was originally adults, but by the end of the 19th century the audience was children. Mr. Punch was supposed to defeat his foes, and be "pleased as punch" the origin of that expression.

Chappell's costume designs were intended for a ballet, but there is no record of whether such a ballet ever was performed.

Costume design for Punch
MEDIUMS: Pencil, ink and watercolor / **DATE:** 1948

▶ **Costume design for Judy**
MEDIUMS: Pencil, ink and watercolor / **DATE:** 1948

Judy

Costume design for Baby

MEDIUMS: Pencil and watercolor / **DATE:** 1948

Costume design for Toby the Dog
MEDIUMS: Pencil, ink and watercolor / **DATE:** 1948

false pockets
done in
stitched on.
white bias binding

POLICEMAN

PUNCH & JUDY
BALLET

Costume design for the Policeman

MEDIUMS: Pencil and watercolor / **DATE:** 1948

Costume design for the Judge

MEDIUMS: Pencil, ink and watercolor / **DATE:** 1948

MAI ZETTERLING
THE
SEAGULL 1949

► **Costume dress design for The Seagull, Act I**
MEDIUMS: Pencil and watercolor / **DATE:** 1949

Mai Elizabeth Zetterling (1925-1994) was born in Sweden. During WWII she began acting in Swedish films. She became a star working for the brilliant director Ingmar Bergman. She moved to England after the war and starred in numerous British films.

"The Seagull" is a play written by the Russian dramatist Anton Chekhov. It was first performed in St. Petersburg, Russia in 1896. English translations were available from 1909 when the play was performed in Glasgow.

The play is written with four acts. Nina is one of the major characters. She lives on an estate in Russia, but her dream is to be an actress. She never achieves great success, but continues to tour with second-rate theatre companies. She is the romantic interest of the two male actors in this play.

THE SEA GULL.
NINA.
MAI ZETTERLING
ACT ONE
WHITE WITH INSETS
OF INSERTION OR
BRODERIE ANGLAIS.

chappell 1949

► **Costume dress design for The Seagull, Act II**
MEDIUMS: Pencil, ink and watercolor / **DATE:** 1949

THE SEAGULL

NINA.

MAI ZETTERLING

ACT II

Sprigg'd or
dotted muslin or
cotton –

Within the image, handwritten annotations read:

THE SEAGULL
NINA.
MAI ZETTERLING
ACT III
Smoke blue with
black braiding

6½ in 54"
9 in 36

Costume dress design for The Seagull, Act III
MEDIUMS: Pencil, ink and watercolor / DATE: 1949

Costume dress design for The Seagull, Act IV
MEDIUMS: Pencil, ink and watercolor / **DATE:** 1949

CALYPSO JOE 1948

Costume design for Calypso Joe
MEDIUMS: Pencil, brush and gouache / **DATE:** 1948

A singer associated with the Caribbean island of Trinidad. He was accompanied by female singers. The group entertained tourists. In 1957 a movie was produced in Hollywood which was entitled "Calypso Joe."

Chappell was associated with the Caribbean since 1935 when he partnered Margot Fonteyn in the ballet "Rio Grande." His post-war interest in a potential ballet was inspired by the success of the Katherine Dunham Dance Company which performed "A Caribbean Rhapsody" in 1948 at the Prince of Wales Theatre, London.

"High Yellow" was a 1932 ballet which included African-American dancer. Chappell did scenery. Burra and Billy had a special interest in Harlem Renaissance, so much so Burra went to NYC in 1934 to visit the people and places in Harlem.

▶ **Costume design for Calypso Joe**
MEDIUMS: Pencil and Watercolor / **DATE:** 1948

FINALE

BARTIRA

Costume design for Calypso Joe

MEDIUMS: Pencil, ink, watercolor and gouache / **DATE:** 1948

Costume design for Calypso Joe
MEDIUMS: Pencil, ink, watercolor and gouache / **DATE:** 1948

Costume design for Calypso Joe

MEDIUMS: Pencil, ink, watercolor and gouache / **DATE:** 1948

Costume design for Calypso Joe
MEDIUMS: Pencil, ink, watercolor and gouache / **DATE:** 1948

Costume design for Calypso Joe

MEDIUMS: Pencil, ink, watercolor and gouache / **DATE:** 1948

FAÇADE
COSTUME DRAWINGS BY WILLIAM CHAPPELL
1949

This ballet was choreographed by Frederick Ashton. It was first performed in April,1931 for the Camargo Society; and then early in May for Ballet Rambert.

The scenery and costumes were designed by John Armstrong. Chappell was one of the lead dancers.

In the spring of 1940, during the period known as the "phoney war", the British Foreign Office decided not to draft the Sadler's Wells male dancers. Instead the entire troupe would be sent to Holland on a goodwill mission.

The troupe arrived on Sunday, May 5th,1940. Performances were held in four cities during the next four days. On each evening they played to packed houses. Their final performance was on Thursday, May 9th. In the early morning hours of May 10th the Germans launched their attacks on Belgium, Holland, and France.

The ballet company spent three horrible days waiting to be evacuated. Finally, on the evening of May 12th they boarded a cargo ship, packed with Dutch refugees. The ship sailed at midnight, and reached England after 15 hours on Monday, May 13th,1940.

All scenery and costumes were abandoned in their haste to leave Holland. Thus, Armstrong's original decor was lost. When Sadler's Wells revived "Façade" for a postwar performance in October 1946 the company created new scenery and costumes. Ashton did not like them.

In 1949 the Sadler's Wells Ballet scheduled a performance of "Façade" at the Royal Opera House to take place on March 2nd,1950. Ashton asked Chappell to draw from memory the original costume designs. Chappell produced detailed drawings, with cast members identified. The drawings show his couture skills as well as his accurate memory.

However, when the ballet was performed the scenery and costumes were credited to John Armstrong, the original designer. Chappell's role was unknown to the audience.

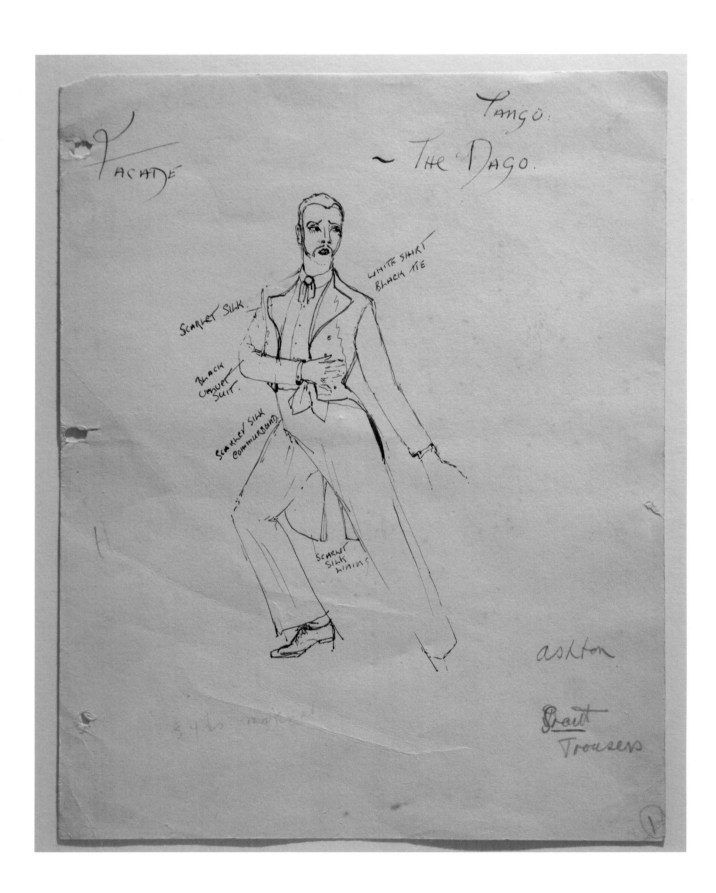

The Dago costume / Designed for Frederick Ashton in the March 1950s Production

Polka costume / Designed for Moira Shearer in the March 1950s Production

Scotch Boy costume / Designed for the March 1950s Production

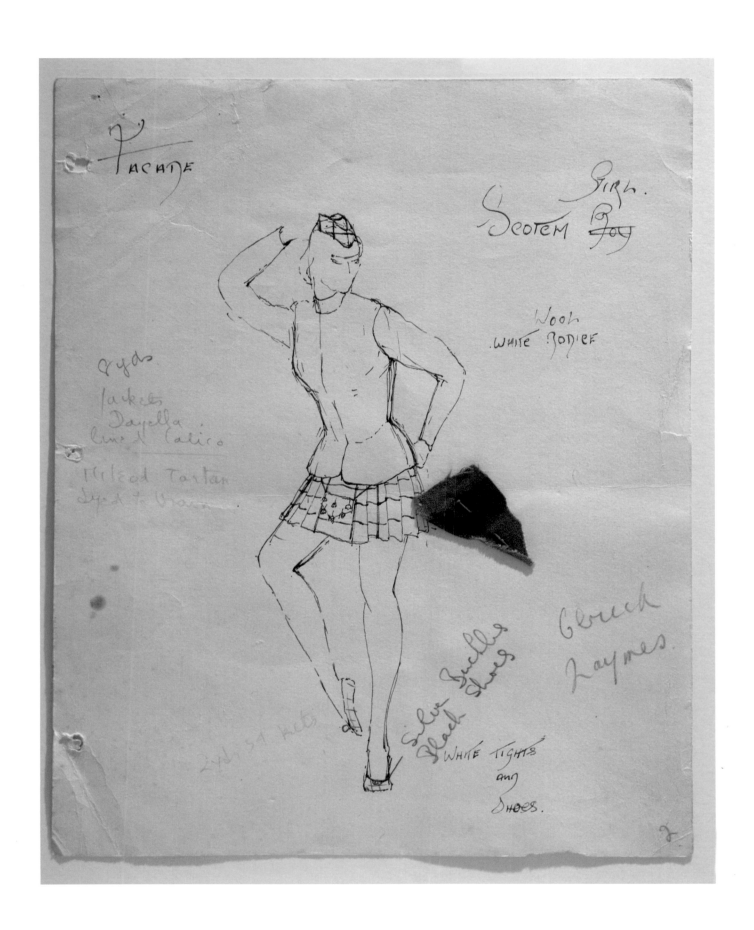

Scotch Girl costume / Designed for the March 1950s Production

Popular Song Boys costume / Designed for Michael Boulton and Donald Britton in the March 1950s Production

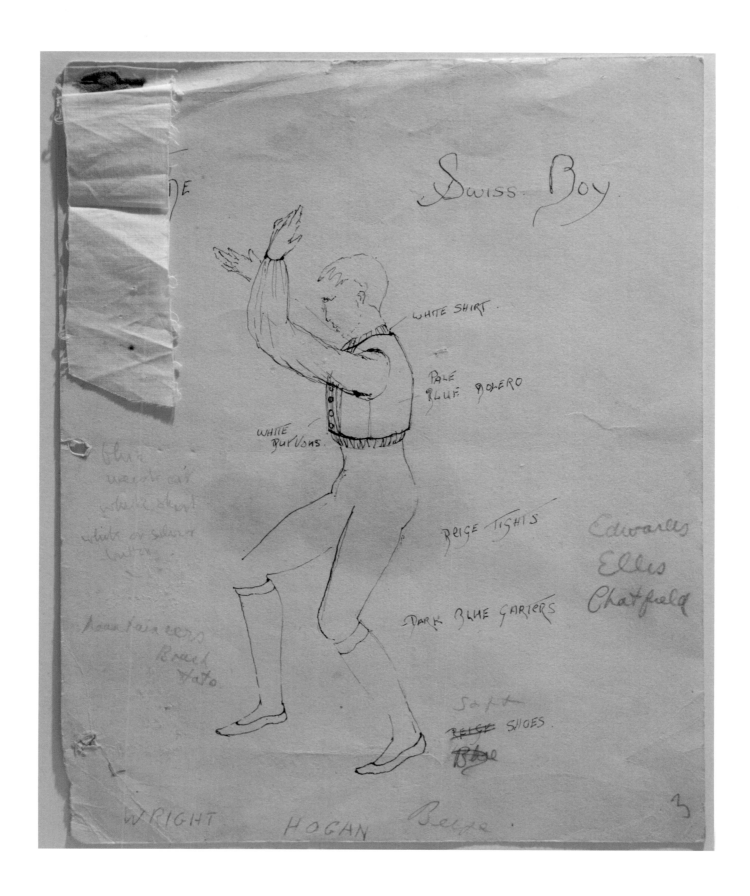

Swiss Boy costume / Designed for the March 1950s Production

BERLIN.
1920.

chappell
1949

BIBLIOGRAPHY

Anthony, Gordon: *Studies of Robert Helpmann*, Home & Van Thal LTD, London 1946

Beaton, Cecil : *Ballet*, Doubleday & Company, Inc., NYC 1951

Bradley, Lionel *Sixteen Years of Ballet Rambert*, Hinrichsen Edition, 1946

Chappell, William: *Well Dearie: The Letters of Edward Burra,* Gordon Fraser Gallery, London, 1985

Chappell, William: *Fonteyn: Impressions of a Ballerina*, Rockliff, London, 1951
                Edward Burra: A Painter Remembered by His Friends, André Deutsch, London, 1982

Daneman, Meredith: *Margot Fonteyn: A Life*, Viking, NYC 2004

De Valois, Ninette: *Come Dance With Me: A Memoir*, London 1957

De Valois, Ninette: *Step by Step,* W.H. Allen, London, 1977

Dolin, Anton: *Markova: Her Life and Art,* Heritage House, NYC, 1953

Dominic, Zoe and Gilbert, John Selwyn: *Frederick Ashton: A Choreographer and His Ballets*, Henry Regnery Company, Chicago, 1973

Fonteyn, Margot: *Autobiography*, W.H. Allen, London, 1975

Haskell, Arnold: *Dancing Around the World"* Dodge, NYC, 1938

Kavanagh, Julie: *Secret Muses: The Life of Frederick Ashton*, Pantheon Books NYC, 1996

Kochno, Boris : *Diaghilev and the Ballets Russes*, Harper & Row, NYC, 1970

Langley-Moore: *June and Doris, The Pleasure of Your Company*, Rich & Cowan, LTD. London, 1936

Motion, Andrew: *The Lamberts" Chat to & Windus*, London, 1986

Markova, Alicia: *Giselle and I*, Viking, NYC, 1960

Rambert, Marie : *Quicksilver-The Autobiography of Marie Rambert*, Macmillan, London, 1972

Scheijen, Sjeng: *Diaghilev: A Life*, Oxford University Press, 2009

Taylor, D.J.: *Bright Young People*, Chatto and Windus, London, 2007

Walker, Kathrine Sorley: *De Basil's Ballets Russes,* Atheneum, NYC, 1983

Walker, Kathrine Sorley: *Ninette De Valois: Idealist Without Illusions*, Hamish Hamilton, London, 1987

◄ Costume design for stage play depicting Berlin in 1920
MEDIUMS: Pencil, ink and watercolor / **DATE:** 1949

American Fashion Art 1960-1990
Three Decades of Advertising Drawings
Frederic A. Sharf with Susan Ward
Format: Softcover **Pages:** 64
ISBN: 978-0-9818865-3-4

The Fashionable Nurse
A Study of Stylish Professional Dressing, 1910-1970
Frederic A. Sharf with Catherine Pate & Jill Carey
Format: Hardcover **Pages:** 64
ISBN: 978-0-9839573-5-5

Larry Salk: California Dreaming
and the Evolution of American Fashion Art: 1945-1965
Frederic A. Sharf with Susan Ward
Format: Softcover **Pages:** 64
ISBN: 1-882266-18-8

Exploring Fashion
The Art of Kenneth Paul Block 1960-1990
Susan Mulcahy with Frederic A. Sharf
Format: Hardcover/Softcover **Pages:** 64
ISBN: Hardcover: 978-0-9818865-7-2
       Softcover: 978-0-9818865-8-9

John Bates: British Fashion Designer
The Sensational Years, 1963-1968
Frederic A. Sharf with Michelle Finamore
Format: Hardcover/Softcover **Pages:** 64
ISBN: Hardcover: 978-0-9839573-6-2
       Softcover: 978-0-9839573-7-9

Style and the City: New York City Fashion Art
Two Decades of Advertising Drawings: 1955-1975
Frederic A. Sharf with Morton Kaish and Alexandra B. Huff
Format: Softcover **Pages:** 72
ISBN: 978-0-9818865-6-5

Beauty as Duty
Textiles on the Homefront of WWII Britain
Alexandra B. Huff with Frederic A. Sharf
Format: Hardcover **Pages:** 80
ISBN: 978-0-9839573-0-0

The Lifestyle of New York Cafe Society, 1935-1950
as Drawn by Jaro Fabry
Frederic A. Sharf
Format: Hardcover **Pages:** 72
ISBN: 978-0-9839573-8-6

Fabric/Figure/Fantasy
Five decades of American fashion drawing (1940s-1980s)
Alexandra B. Huff and Frederic A. Sharf
with Phil French and Morton Kaish
Format: Hardcover **Pages:** 104
ISBN: 978-0-9839573-1-7

Louis Féron Master Jeweler 1901-1998
Paris, Costa Rica, New York
Emily Banis Stoehrer and Frederic A. Sharf
Format: Hardcover **Pages:** 80
ISBN: 978-0-9839573-4-8

Brian Stonehouse, MBE: 1918-1998
Artist, Soldier, War Hero, Fashion Illustrator
Frederic A. Sharf
Format: Hardcover **Pages:** 64
ISBN: 978-0-9903152-1-6

business unfinished, fill his purse wickedly with the ill-gotten wealth which he had taken from the Church, despoiling both realms with his deceit.

Hearing all this, the bishop of Amiens was enraged. He rose to his feet and there in open court, with indescribable arrogance, he pointed his finger at the pope, replying with these wrathful words: 'Archbishop of Bari, you are lying!' Then he swept out of the consistory and departed insolently from the pope's presence. A number of the cardinals followed him, some because they agreed with him, others because they were guilty of similar misdeeds. The pope immediately stripped them of their offices, and appointed others to take their place, twenty-nine in all, men of great excellence from various realms, archbishops, bishops and archdeacons.

After these events, the apostate cardinals dared to stir up open war against the pope, and they determined to pursue him and his supporters to the death. To strengthen their cause, they chose as Pope Clement VII a well-born Frenchman, who was related by blood to the king of France.

1379

In parliament at London, with the connivance of certain persons who were always working out some harmful scheme, a new tax [the poll tax] was decreed for the use of King Richard. The house of lords forbore to bring this proposal before the commons, who had been almost overcome by earlier exactions. The dukes of Lancaster and Brittany were to pay twenty marks, that is ten marks apiece, and the archbishops the same. The earls were each to pay six marks, as were the bishops and the mitred abbots, and what is more the abbots were obliged to pay forty pence per head for their monks.

The regulations for the collection of the tax showed clearly that those who had devised them lacked good judgement, for the poorest abbot was bound to contribute as much by reason of his headgear as the richest of the earls and bishops, and more on top of that for his monks, so that his total liability would exceed that of the dukes.

The great schism

THE great schism lasted for 39 years, from 1378 to 1417, during which there was no one universally recognized pope. For the previous seven decades, since 1309, the papacy had been based at Avignon, despite many appeals to return to Rome: it was widely believed that the Avignon popes, living close to France and mostly French-born, were under the thumb of the French monarchy. But not until 1376 did Gregory XI move the papal court back to the Eternal City.

When Gregory died in 1378, the college of cardinals that met to elect his successor was split into three parties: unable to elect a pope with the required two-thirds majority, the cardinals selected an outsider – Bartolomeo Prignano, archbishop of Bari, Italian by nationality but French in education and outlook. The mob broke in, however, clamouring for a Roman pope, and to pacify them, the cardinals pretended to have elected the aged Roman Cardinal Tibaldeschi. Once the crowd had departed, and after the college had moved to the fortified papal palace at Anagni, a place of greater safety, they proclaimed Archbishop Prignano as Pope Urban VI.

Severe and ascetic, Urban VI detested clerical luxury and its attendant sins, and was determined to reform the Church – starting with the cardinals. He also possessed a violent temper, a tendency to sadism, and an obscene vocabulary, and before long the combination of his shocking behaviour and his plans for reform convinced the cardinals they had made a disastrous choice. They withdrew to Anagni, where they deposed Urban, declaring that, because he had been chosen only through fear of the mob, his election was invalid. The college proclaimed the French cardinal, Robert of Geneva, as Pope Clement